If found, please contact:

_____

_____

This log contains records for the following time period:

____/____ to ____/____

Copyright © 2019 by Simply Pretty Log Books
All rights reserved. This book or any portion thereof may not be reproduced or used in any manner whatsoever without the express written permission of the publisher except for the use of brief quotations in a book review.

MILEAGE LOG

MAKE:		MODEL:		YEAR:	
DATE:	ODOMETER: START | END		TOTAL:	DESTINATION / PURPOSE:	

MILEAGE LOG

MAKE:		MODEL:		YEAR:	
DATE:		ODOMETER: START | END		TOTAL:	DESTINATION / PURPOSE:

MILEAGE LOG

MAKE:		MODEL:		YEAR:	
DATE:	ODOMETER: START | END		TOTAL:	DESTINATION / PURPOSE:	

MILEAGE LOG

MAKE:		MODEL:		YEAR:	
DATE:		ODOMETER: START | END		TOTAL:	DESTINATION / PURPOSE:

MILEAGE LOG

MAKE:		MODEL:		YEAR:	
DATE:	ODOMETER: START | END		TOTAL:	DESTINATION / PURPOSE:	

MILEAGE LOG

MAKE:		MODEL:		YEAR:	
DATE:		ODOMETER: START | END		TOTAL:	DESTINATION / PURPOSE:

MILEAGE LOG

MAKE:		MODEL:		YEAR:	
DATE:		ODOMETER: START | END		TOTAL:	DESTINATION / PURPOSE:

MILEAGE LOG

MAKE:		MODEL:		YEAR:	
DATE:	ODOMETER: START | END		TOTAL:	DESTINATION / PURPOSE:	

MILEAGE LOG

MAKE:		MODEL:		YEAR:	
DATE:	ODOMETER: START | END		TOTAL:	DESTINATION / PURPOSE:	

MILEAGE LOG

MAKE:		MODEL:		YEAR:	
DATE:		ODOMETER: START | END		TOTAL:	DESTINATION / PURPOSE:

MILEAGE LOG

MAKE:		MODEL:		YEAR:	
DATE:	ODOMETER: START | END		TOTAL:	DESTINATION / PURPOSE:	

MILEAGE LOG

MAKE:		MODEL:		YEAR:	
DATE:		ODOMETER: START | END		TOTAL:	DESTINATION / PURPOSE:

MILEAGE LOG

MAKE:		MODEL:		YEAR:	
DATE:	ODOMETER: START | END		TOTAL:	DESTINATION / PURPOSE:	

MILEAGE LOG

MAKE:		MODEL:		YEAR:	
DATE:	ODOMETER: START | END		TOTAL:	DESTINATION / PURPOSE:	

MILEAGE LOG

MAKE:		MODEL:		YEAR:	
DATE:	ODOMETER: START | END		TOTAL:	DESTINATION / PURPOSE:	

MILEAGE LOG

MAKE:		MODEL:		YEAR:	
DATE:	ODOMETER: START | END		TOTAL:	DESTINATION / PURPOSE:	

MILEAGE LOG

MAKE:		MODEL:		YEAR:	
DATE:	ODOMETER: START | END		TOTAL:	DESTINATION / PURPOSE:	

MILEAGE LOG

MAKE:		MODEL:		YEAR:	
DATE:		ODOMETER: START | END		TOTAL:	DESTINATION / PURPOSE:

MILEAGE LOG

MAKE:		MODEL:		YEAR:	
DATE:		ODOMETER: START | END		TOTAL:	DESTINATION / PURPOSE:

MILEAGE LOG

MAKE:		MODEL:		YEAR:	
DATE:		ODOMETER: START | END		TOTAL:	DESTINATION / PURPOSE:

MILEAGE LOG

MAKE:		MODEL:		YEAR:	
DATE:	ODOMETER: START | END		TOTAL:	DESTINATION / PURPOSE:	

MILEAGE LOG

MAKE:		MODEL:		YEAR:	
DATE:	ODOMETER: START | END		TOTAL:	DESTINATION / PURPOSE:	

MILEAGE LOG

MAKE:		MODEL:		YEAR:
DATE:	ODOMETER: START | END		TOTAL:	DESTINATION / PURPOSE:

MILEAGE LOG

MAKE:		MODEL:		YEAR:	
DATE:		ODOMETER: START | END		TOTAL:	DESTINATION / PURPOSE:

MILEAGE LOG

MAKE:		MODEL:		YEAR:	
DATE:	ODOMETER: START | END		TOTAL:	DESTINATION / PURPOSE:	

MILEAGE LOG

MAKE:		MODEL:		YEAR:	
DATE:		ODOMETER: START | END		TOTAL:	DESTINATION / PURPOSE:

MILEAGE LOG

MAKE:		MODEL:		YEAR:	
DATE:	ODOMETER: START | END		TOTAL:	DESTINATION / PURPOSE:	

MILEAGE LOG

MAKE:		MODEL:		YEAR:	
DATE:		ODOMETER: START | END		TOTAL:	DESTINATION / PURPOSE:

MILEAGE LOG

MAKE:		MODEL:		YEAR:	
DATE:		ODOMETER: START | END		TOTAL:	DESTINATION / PURPOSE:

MILEAGE LOG

MAKE:		MODEL:		YEAR:	
DATE:		ODOMETER: START | END		TOTAL:	DESTINATION / PURPOSE:

MILEAGE LOG

MAKE:		MODEL:		YEAR:	
DATE:	ODOMETER: START | END		TOTAL:	DESTINATION / PURPOSE:	

MILEAGE LOG

MAKE:		MODEL:		YEAR:	
DATE:		ODOMETER: START | END		TOTAL:	DESTINATION / PURPOSE:

MILEAGE LOG

MAKE:		MODEL:		YEAR:	
DATE:	ODOMETER: START | END		TOTAL:	DESTINATION / PURPOSE:	

MILEAGE LOG

MAKE:		MODEL:		YEAR:	
DATE:		ODOMETER: START | END		TOTAL:	DESTINATION / PURPOSE:

MILEAGE LOG

MAKE:		MODEL:		YEAR:	
DATE:	ODOMETER: START | END		TOTAL:	DESTINATION / PURPOSE:	

MILEAGE LOG

MAKE:		MODEL:		YEAR:	
DATE:		ODOMETER: START | END		TOTAL:	DESTINATION / PURPOSE:

MILEAGE LOG

MAKE:		MODEL:		YEAR:	
DATE:	ODOMETER: START | END		TOTAL:	DESTINATION / PURPOSE:	

MILEAGE LOG

MAKE:		MODEL:		YEAR:	
DATE:		ODOMETER: START | END		TOTAL:	DESTINATION / PURPOSE:

MILEAGE LOG

MAKE:		MODEL:		YEAR:	
DATE:	ODOMETER: START | END		TOTAL:	DESTINATION / PURPOSE:	

MILEAGE LOG

MAKE:		MODEL:		YEAR:	
DATE:	ODOMETER: START | END		TOTAL:	DESTINATION / PURPOSE:	

MILEAGE LOG

MAKE:		MODEL:		YEAR:	
DATE:	ODOMETER: START | END		TOTAL:	DESTINATION / PURPOSE:	

MILEAGE LOG

MAKE:		MODEL:		YEAR:	
DATE:		ODOMETER: START | END		TOTAL:	DESTINATION / PURPOSE:

MILEAGE LOG

MAKE:		MODEL:		YEAR:	
DATE:	ODOMETER: START | END		TOTAL:	DESTINATION / PURPOSE:	

MILEAGE LOG

MAKE:		MODEL:		YEAR:	
DATE:		ODOMETER: START | END		TOTAL:	DESTINATION / PURPOSE:

MILEAGE LOG

MAKE:		MODEL:		YEAR:	
DATE:	ODOMETER: START | END		TOTAL:	DESTINATION / PURPOSE:	

MILEAGE LOG

MAKE:		MODEL:		YEAR:	
DATE:		ODOMETER: START | END		TOTAL:	DESTINATION / PURPOSE:

MILEAGE LOG

MAKE:		MODEL:		YEAR:	
DATE:		ODOMETER: START | END		TOTAL:	DESTINATION / PURPOSE:

MILEAGE LOG

MAKE:		MODEL:		YEAR:	
DATE:		ODOMETER: START | END		TOTAL:	DESTINATION / PURPOSE:

MILEAGE LOG

MAKE:		MODEL:		YEAR:	
DATE:	ODOMETER: START | END		TOTAL:	DESTINATION / PURPOSE:	

MILEAGE LOG

MAKE:		MODEL:		YEAR:	
DATE:		ODOMETER: START | END		TOTAL:	DESTINATION / PURPOSE:

MILEAGE LOG

MAKE:		MODEL:		YEAR:	
DATE:	ODOMETER: START | END		TOTAL:	DESTINATION / PURPOSE:	

MILEAGE LOG

MAKE:		MODEL:		YEAR:	
DATE:		ODOMETER: START | END		TOTAL:	DESTINATION / PURPOSE:

MILEAGE LOG

MAKE:		MODEL:		YEAR:	
DATE:	ODOMETER: START | END		TOTAL:	DESTINATION / PURPOSE:	

MILEAGE LOG

MAKE:		MODEL:		YEAR:	
DATE:		ODOMETER: START | END		TOTAL:	DESTINATION / PURPOSE:

MILEAGE LOG

MAKE:		MODEL:		YEAR:	
DATE:	ODOMETER: START | END		TOTAL:	DESTINATION / PURPOSE:	

MILEAGE LOG

MAKE:		MODEL:		YEAR:	
DATE:		ODOMETER: START | END		TOTAL:	DESTINATION / PURPOSE:

MILEAGE LOG

MAKE:		MODEL:		YEAR:	
DATE:	ODOMETER: START | END		TOTAL:	DESTINATION / PURPOSE:	

MILEAGE LOG

MAKE:		MODEL:		YEAR:	
DATE:		ODOMETER: START | END		TOTAL:	DESTINATION / PURPOSE:

MILEAGE LOG

MAKE:		MODEL:		YEAR:	
DATE:	ODOMETER: START | END		TOTAL:	DESTINATION / PURPOSE:	

MILEAGE LOG

MAKE:		MODEL:		YEAR:	
DATE:		ODOMETER: START | END		TOTAL:	DESTINATION / PURPOSE:

MILEAGE LOG

MAKE:		MODEL:		YEAR:	
DATE:	ODOMETER: START | END		TOTAL:	DESTINATION / PURPOSE:	

MILEAGE LOG

MAKE:		MODEL:		YEAR:	
DATE:		ODOMETER: START | END		TOTAL:	DESTINATION / PURPOSE:

MILEAGE LOG

MAKE:		MODEL:		YEAR:	
DATE:		ODOMETER: START | END		TOTAL:	DESTINATION / PURPOSE:

MILEAGE LOG

MAKE:		MODEL:		YEAR:	
DATE:		ODOMETER: START | END		TOTAL:	DESTINATION / PURPOSE:

MILEAGE LOG

MAKE:		MODEL:		YEAR:	
DATE:	ODOMETER: START | END		TOTAL:	DESTINATION / PURPOSE:	

MILEAGE LOG

MAKE:		MODEL:		YEAR:	
DATE:		ODOMETER: START | END		TOTAL:	DESTINATION / PURPOSE:

MILEAGE LOG

MAKE:		MODEL:		YEAR:	
DATE:	ODOMETER: START | END		TOTAL:	DESTINATION / PURPOSE:	

MILEAGE LOG

MAKE:		MODEL:		YEAR:	
DATE:	ODOMETER: START | END		TOTAL:	DESTINATION / PURPOSE:	

MILEAGE LOG

MAKE:		MODEL:		YEAR:	
DATE:	ODOMETER: START | END		TOTAL:	DESTINATION / PURPOSE:	

MILEAGE LOG

MAKE:		MODEL:		YEAR:	
DATE:		ODOMETER: START | END		TOTAL:	DESTINATION / PURPOSE:

MILEAGE LOG

MAKE:		MODEL:		YEAR:	
DATE:	ODOMETER: START | END		TOTAL:	DESTINATION / PURPOSE:	

MILEAGE LOG

MAKE:		MODEL:		YEAR:	
DATE:		ODOMETER: START | END		TOTAL:	DESTINATION / PURPOSE:

MILEAGE LOG

MAKE:		MODEL:		YEAR:	
DATE:	ODOMETER: START | END		TOTAL:	DESTINATION / PURPOSE:	

MILEAGE LOG

MAKE:		MODEL:		YEAR:	
DATE:	**ODOMETER: START | END**		**TOTAL:**	**DESTINATION / PURPOSE:**	

MILEAGE LOG

MAKE:		MODEL:		YEAR:	
DATE:	ODOMETER: START | END		TOTAL:	DESTINATION / PURPOSE:	

MILEAGE LOG

MAKE:		MODEL:		YEAR:	
DATE:		ODOMETER: START | END		TOTAL:	DESTINATION / PURPOSE:

MILEAGE LOG

MAKE:		MODEL:		YEAR:	
DATE:	ODOMETER: START | END		TOTAL:	DESTINATION / PURPOSE:	

MILEAGE LOG

MAKE:		MODEL:		YEAR:	
DATE:	ODOMETER: START | END		TOTAL:	DESTINATION / PURPOSE:	

MILEAGE LOG

MAKE:		MODEL:		YEAR:	
DATE:		ODOMETER: START | END		TOTAL:	DESTINATION / PURPOSE:

MILEAGE LOG

MAKE:		MODEL:		YEAR:	
DATE:		ODOMETER: START | END		TOTAL:	DESTINATION / PURPOSE:

MILEAGE LOG

MAKE:		MODEL:		YEAR:	
DATE:		ODOMETER: START | END		TOTAL:	DESTINATION / PURPOSE:

MILEAGE LOG

MAKE:		MODEL:		YEAR:
DATE:	ODOMETER: START | END		TOTAL:	DESTINATION / PURPOSE:

MILEAGE LOG

MAKE:		MODEL:		YEAR:	
DATE:	ODOMETER: START | END		TOTAL:	DESTINATION / PURPOSE:	

MILEAGE LOG

MAKE:		MODEL:		YEAR:	
DATE:		ODOMETER: START | END		TOTAL:	DESTINATION / PURPOSE:

MILEAGE LOG

MAKE:		MODEL:		YEAR:	
DATE:	ODOMETER: START | END		TOTAL:	DESTINATION / PURPOSE:	

MILEAGE LOG

MAKE:		MODEL:		YEAR:	
DATE:		ODOMETER: START | END		TOTAL:	DESTINATION / PURPOSE:

MILEAGE LOG

MAKE:		MODEL:		YEAR:	
DATE:	ODOMETER: START | END		TOTAL:	DESTINATION / PURPOSE:	

MILEAGE LOG

MAKE:		MODEL:		YEAR:	
DATE:		ODOMETER: START | END		TOTAL:	DESTINATION / PURPOSE:

MILEAGE LOG

MAKE:		MODEL:		YEAR:	
DATE:		ODOMETER: START | END		TOTAL:	DESTINATION / PURPOSE:

MILEAGE LOG

MAKE:		MODEL:		YEAR:	
DATE:		ODOMETER: START | END		TOTAL:	DESTINATION / PURPOSE:

MILEAGE LOG

MAKE:		MODEL:		YEAR:	
DATE:	ODOMETER: START | END		TOTAL:	DESTINATION / PURPOSE:	

MILEAGE LOG

MAKE:		MODEL:		YEAR:	
DATE:		ODOMETER: START | END		TOTAL:	DESTINATION / PURPOSE:

MILEAGE LOG

MAKE:		MODEL:		YEAR:	
DATE:	ODOMETER: START | END		TOTAL:	DESTINATION / PURPOSE:	

MILEAGE LOG

MAKE:		MODEL:		YEAR:	
DATE:		ODOMETER: START | END		TOTAL:	DESTINATION / PURPOSE:

MILEAGE LOG

MAKE:		MODEL:		YEAR:	
DATE:	ODOMETER: START | END		TOTAL:	DESTINATION / PURPOSE:	

MILEAGE LOG

MAKE:		MODEL:		YEAR:	
DATE:		ODOMETER: START | END		TOTAL:	DESTINATION / PURPOSE:

MILEAGE LOG

MAKE:		MODEL:		YEAR:	
DATE:	ODOMETER: START | END		TOTAL:	DESTINATION / PURPOSE:	

MILEAGE LOG

MAKE:		MODEL:		YEAR:	
DATE:		ODOMETER: START | END		TOTAL:	DESTINATION / PURPOSE:

MILEAGE LOG

MAKE:		MODEL:		YEAR:	
DATE:	ODOMETER: START | END		TOTAL:	DESTINATION / PURPOSE:	

MILEAGE LOG

MAKE:		MODEL:		YEAR:	
DATE:		ODOMETER: START | END		TOTAL:	DESTINATION / PURPOSE:

www.ingramcontent.com/pod-product-compliance
Lightning Source LLC
Chambersburg PA
CBHW070426220526
45466CB00004B/1559